OUT OF THIS WORLD

Imagination Of Words

Edited By Jenni Harrison

First published in Great Britain in 2020 by:

Young Writers
Remus House
Coltsfoot Drive
Peterborough
PE2 9BF
Telephone: 01733 890066
Website: www.youngwriters.co.uk

Book Design by Ashley Janson

Softback ISBN 978-1-80015-003-4

Printed and bound in the UK by BookPrintingUK
Website: www.bookprintinguk.com
YB0446S

FOREWORD

Here at Young Writers our defining aim is to promote the joys of reading and writing to children and young adults and we are committed to nurturing the creative talents of the next generation. By allowing them to see their own work in print we believe their confidence and love of creative writing will grow.

Out Of This World is our latest fantastic competition, specifically designed to encourage the writing skills of primary school children through the medium of poetry. From the high quality of entries received, it is clear that it really captured the imagination of all involved.

We are proud to present the resulting collection of poems that we are sure will amuse and inspire.

An absorbing insight into the imagination and thoughts of the young, we hope you will agree that this fantastic anthology is one to delight the whole family again and again.

CONTENTS

Maldon Primary School, Maldon

Our Lady's Catholic Primary School, Cowley

St Alfege With St Peter's CE Primary School, Greenwich

St George's Cathedral Catholic Primary School, Southwark

THE POEMS

The First Dog In Space

As Laika goes to space
She meets a sausage dog
When she misses her lovely place
She finds an unknown bog

She sees passing comets
She has an alien cheetah chasing her
Trying to get her beautiful bonnets
Uh oh! Her rockets are out of fuel!

The galaxy is a spacious place
Wonder where humans are
She loves space but her rocket got filled with tar

Space is so much more
It is unending
It is the key to Laika's door
You, in space, will never be unfriendly

Laika is an astronaut
With space antennae
She is very much taught
Now her rocket is burning.

Syprinne Gwedeza-Zulu (9)
Brunswick Park Primary School, Camberwell

My Friendship With Winter

P laying in the snow is fun but not in ice
L oving, kind smiles fill the air
A little bit of warmth would be nice
Y ou can't bring the blizzard of snow
I cicles hang like cobwebs upon the snowy house
N o small, green shoot will pop up from under the ice
G orgeous winter can't you bring us at least a grouse?

F rosty happiness of winter stole my heart
R oofs full of snow and frost
I nside me is a child still young and smart
E verlasting sparkle of icicles
N ow the river cannot flow
D eer leaping with joy
S ilvery showers of snow.

W ater turning to ice
I n your unfriendly attempt
N ot to turn everywhere to paradise
T ree house with broken ladders
E xcited people paying their price
R oofs full of melting snow
S parkle of ice

F reezing shivering sun
A nd does with the winter's child
M ay will soon come
I cy crystal eyes staring at me
L osing unique, silvery snowflakes all getting old
Y ou are trying to rhyme, snap of cold.

Eve Loune (9)
Brunswick Park Primary School, Camberwell

The Winter Poem

Racing over the snowy, beautiful landscape
Wearing wooden, long skis
Leaping so high
I could imagine myself touching the sky

Winter breeze everywhere I go
Squeezing my shoes through the snow
My boots nearly freezing up in ice
A little hot chill would be nice

My friend the winter child by my side
Us playing singalongs right outside
The animals all coming to watch
See us playing in the notch

Mum cuddling me up all warm
Me getting scared because of the storm
My grandma getting sicker and sicker in the night
Come on Gran, you need to fight.

Shammah Mahile (9)
Brunswick Park Primary School, Camberwell

Snow Day

Playing over the snowy fields
Loving the small wonderful icicles on me
And I love snow! Wow!
Yeah! Snowing every day
In the winter I play
Never stop playing on my skis
Going in and out every day

Winter! Wow!
I love to play in the snow
No one could ever stop me
Today is the day
Every day I play
Racing with my skis

Friends!
Racing to my friend
In the snow, I play
My friend is nice
Next to him, I play
I would like to tell you his name
But, anonymous he shall stay.

Marliatou Sow (9)
Brunswick Park Primary School, Camberwell

Snow And Stars

Tiny unique snowflakes falling on the ground
A boy with crystal-blue eyes
Deer with pointy antlers
A boy wearing skis with a big size

A roof with shining snow
A basket with wooden skis
A hill with shining ice
I walk with ease

Deer with crystal-black eyes
Small happy doe
Huge tree of ice
The deer stand below

A snap of cold
Abandoned unused tree house
A tree with broken branches
A doe acts like Mickey Mouse

I sit under the sky
Looking at the stars
I wave the sky goodbye
As I walk away looking at the stars.

Joel Avdyli (9)
Brunswick Park Primary School, Camberwell

Humans Vs Monsters

One dark night
I woke up the sound of my family screaming
I rushed out of bed, put on my shoes
And glanced out of the window and saw...
Aliens, witches, anything you could imagine
Destroying our world
I was too scared to go
But some passion fled
Through me telling me to fight for my right
So I kicked the door open
And figured out the power was coming for the core!
So I smashed the core, took out the jewel
And broke it.
So before I knew it
The monsters disappeared into a hole
And everything was normal!

Emily Boye (9)
Brunswick Park Primary School, Camberwell

Monster Adventure

We're in space at 100 pace
In our rocket looking for monsters
Going everywhere
Then we went to the coldest planet
Which is -225 degrees
Then we see something strange
In the distance around space
We go closer and we see it
A monster king
As ugly as can be
Like a disgusting piggy
And we know it's a king
Because it's got six rings
As strong as a dinosaur
Trying to get closer
But he's throwing rocks at us
Then we decide to go back home.

Noah Meftah Cunningham (8)
Brunswick Park Primary School, Camberwell

Winter Happiness

Freezing, shivering boy
Frosty, wintery snow
Snap of cold

Drip of snow
Boy with animals
Deer with winter's child

Happy, excited grin of Grandma
Loving, kind smile of Mum
Frosty happiness of air

Chill of air
Tree with broken branches
Tree house with broken ladder

Unique silvery snowflakes
Icy crystal eyes
Leap of the deer

Happiness of winter
Blizzard of snowflakes
Mountain of snow.

Harmony Daniels (9)
Brunswick Park Primary School, Camberwell

Astronauts

A stronauts up in space
S limy green aliens attack
T hrowing spaceships into space
R eady, steady, up they go
O ver there we see planets
N ever go to the dark side
A mazing twinkling stars are shining
U nhappy aliens lose their bright green spaceship
T rying to find their way home
S urprised astronauts when they finally land back
on Earth.

Malachi Abioye (9), N'Kiyah-Star, Adam Pearson (8), Shayla Ferguson (8) & Jamie Walcott (8)
Brunswick Park Primary School, Camberwell

The Merciless Phoenix

People are afraid of that
Ham eating monster
Escape from it while you have the chance
It's worse than dying from a blaster

The phoenix lurks in the dark
If it scratches you it will make a mark
Sees you and you're dead
He'll make you into bread

Do you like apple pie
Well that's you when you die
It's more vicious than a shark
All the way from Iraq.

Qoyhum Onafowokan (9)
Brunswick Park Primary School, Camberwell

Harry Potter

H iding in the night I saw Dobby
A nd he looked like a copy
R eady to fly about on a broomstick
R eady, one, two, three, going to pick
Y eah I love it up here

P icking my broom
O nce I picked soon
T ingling with fear
T ight and clear
E very night I see Voldemort
R eady to be reunited.

Wendy Oliveira (9)
Brunswick Park Primary School, Camberwell

The Haunted House

Ding dong
I know where you're hiding
You can keep me finding
You can lock your door
Shut
Shut
Shut
Shut
Ding dong
I know where you're hiding
You can't stop me finding
Just a piece of cake to start off
I can come from here
I can come from there
I can come from anywhere
Ding dong
I found you
Ha ha!

Aisha Kamara (8)
Brunswick Park Primary School, Camberwell

Pizza

The nice delicious cheese on top of the yummy pizza
The dry cheesy crust above the yummy pizza
The pizza shaped into delicious triangles
The yummy topping sinking into
The glorious, the amazing, the fantastic cheese
The spectacular cheese
What is on top of the pizza?
The healthy tomato sauce
Beneath the melty cheese
The amazing pizza.

Roman Powell (9)
Brunswick Park Primary School, Camberwell

True Moonlight

Stars so bright
Shimmering in the night
So delicate, just like snow
Glaring at the stars
Makes me smile

I could see a crescent moon
Shaped like a boomerang
Can't wait
To see Saturn

A ring
Shaped like a wheel
The touch of the surface
Makes me tingle!

Fawaz Ajani (9)
Brunswick Park Primary School, Camberwell

Flying To Space

I went to fly to space
My parents thought it was a disgrace
I love space
I love the planets most

Behind me was a planet
It was my favourite colour
It was Mars
I love Mars

I went to fly to space
My parents thought it was a disgrace
I enjoyed space
I enjoyed Mars.

Oliver Underhill (8)
Brunswick Park Primary School, Camberwell

I'm A Winter Boy

Finally it is winter
I am a boy who loves winter
All the snow falling down
There is no need for a frown

I'm going out to make a snowman
I've found a friend to play with
My nana calls me back
And I play with my train track.

Reece Hubball (8)
Brunswick Park Primary School, Camberwell

Save The Koalas

Koalas are cute, Australia is due
Fires are new
But there is not much stew.

Save the koalas
Love them, don't judge them
I came to Australie to save them
Not hate them.

Saratou Kamara (8)
Brunswick Park Primary School, Camberwell

A Poem Of Space

Space is an infinite vacuum
It stretches out further than every fume
The stars shine bright
And the planets spin with might
The sun burns as it glows
Do you think it will explode?
We just don't know
It might blow
Now, in 1962
J F Kennedy wanted America to go to the moon
It happened very soon
The mission was called Apollo 11
And how many years it took exactly
Seven - I think
The President's speech was spoken in 1962
And take off was in 1969
That took some time
Where were we?
Oh, the stars
Did you know the sun isn't the biggest star?
There is one far

A star bigger than all the stars
The red hyper giant
It must be giant
The planets so vast
I don't know where to start
There's Mercury, Venus, Earth, Mars
Jupiter, Saturn, Uranus, Neptune
And the dwarf planet Pluto
Our moon is the achievement we've reached
But we can reach a bigger feat
Tell me what you think
Next is extraterrestrial life
That would be nice!
Bye!

Summer Wallis (10)
Copnor Primary School, Portsmouth

The Boy Who Loved The Moon

There was a little boy who loved the moon
He had them in his room
When he went to school
He told everyone about it
It was his birthday soon
The class wanted to know what to get him
They had an idea
And soon everyone could hear
So next morning
When the boy came to the classroom
He could see amazing beautiful moons
Everywhere in the room
The boy was the happiest boy in the world.

Pola Zimoch (9)
Copnor Primary School, Portsmouth

Space Mission

S parkling stars
P eople floating
A s light as a feather
C ommander Neil Armstrong
E xtraordinary mission

Space is full of beautiful colours
Black, orange and blue
Maybe one day you can see it too
A magnificent universe waiting out there for you
But for now just admire the view!

Bella Johnson (10)
Copnor Primary School, Portsmouth

My Brother Klaus

I live in a house
With my brother Klaus
He stares at the stars
While I eat chocolate bars
I love him so
But he prefers Mo
So I hang with Josie
Who's really nosy
What happened to Klaus I should've known
So now I let him be all on his own.

Isabelle Overy (10)
Copnor Primary School, Portsmouth

The Jewellery Shop

I compressed my face against the glass
I was hypnotised by the glimmering mass
It pulled me in, the pearls and rings
All of this was the wealth of kings
The eternity of money and worth
Like the beautiful sun that shines in Perth
I am nearly blinded by the shimmer
The light and the colour let off a beauteous glimmer
As my mum dragged me away into the bleak street
I said that shop was neat
We travelled home that cold evening
I knew that shop held special meaning
In the jewellery shop fancy and well
Had a story to tell
Where beauty is not all that matters
It does not have a care if your clothes have tatters
You are you on the inside!

Hudson Williams (11)
Maldon Court Preparatory School, Maldon

D-Day

The cramped boat had stiffened my joints,
The beach was as dark as mud.
Our commander gave some points,
Before a bullet made his head spill blood.
Screams and shots made my ears bleed,
I got a knife to my arm from the barrel of a gun.
Some medication I did need,
But my killer was having some fun.
I took out my back-up pistol
As he loaded his Thompson,
I became as pale as a crystal,
And did my only option.
I kicked him to the ground, as he gave a cry,
I shot his head and I shot his thigh.
He fell lifeless to the ground,
I got back up but fell back down.
I stayed, wishing for help, but heard not a sound.
I gripped my arm and woke up,
I was in a bleak white bed,
A bandage was on my shoulder,
A plaster on my head.

A slip of paper was on a bedside table,
I lifted my head and read
You were stabbed,
And soon you will be dead.

Harry Scott (11)
Maldon Court Preparatory School, Maldon

Suzy Groppy

The chief defect of Suzy Groppy
Was that at school she would always copy

As she sat in the class
She would make such a face

For over a shoulder she would look
At what was in her neighbour's book

For one day her neighbour grew wise
And in her work was a surprise

For she had written everything wrong
And actually written a very long song

The answers were not there for Suzy to copy
Suddenly Suzy went quite floppy

The shock of it all, very wrong
Had made her stomach cause a pong

The whole class did laugh
But Suzy needed a big bath.

William Bruce (9)
Maldon Court Preparatory School, Maldon

Winter Days

Warm, cosy houses are filled with an aroma of hot chocolate
Santa jumping from house to house to house, delivering children's dreams
Family members gather together singing Christmas carols
Mums preparing a roast dinner
Children forming snow angels in the pale snow.

Snow falling like tears in the eyes
Families ice skating in Central Park
Coffee shops packed with school mums
School children wearing duffle coats
Reindeer footsteps clitter clattering on the roofs

Schools instantly closing
The moonlight comes out before it's supposed to
Here comes spring.

Giselle Kikaroboka (11)
Maldon Court Preparatory School, Maldon

Gaming Grace

There once was a girl called Grace
Who had a shock when she saw her face

What her parents had said had come true
Her face had turned blue

Now let me tell you of this terrible state
That poor Grace found did not abate

Everybody laughed at her which Grace found unfair
It was as if they didn't really care

All the time she spent inside
Meant her skin could not abide

The healthy glow it once had shown
Had turned a dreadful blue tone

For now Grace cared about the air
She was sad that people would just stare.

Kate van Stolk (10)
Maldon Court Preparatory School, Maldon

Treasure

All these unique things around me
Could be the answer to my life
Pacing around like a ginger cat
Trying to find the treasure I've been waiting for
Jewels glistening in the sun as they catch my eye
Just thinking about all that gold
Feels like I have control over everybody
As I jog back to my patched den
I realise what an amazing thing I have found
It is a ring (and a blingy one too)
I hop up and down like a bunny with excitement
If I sell this amazing object
I could make a fortune
And never be ignored again.

Louisa Rainger (11)
Maldon Court Preparatory School, Maldon

Cautionary Tale

The chief defect of Steve Strife
Who only ate sweets for all his life
He never thought about the world around
He only heard the sound
Of the sweet packet opening *rip!*
From then on he was called Sugary Steve as he licked his lips
It led to a dreadful fate
The story I will now relate
One day he ate so much
He felt his stomach clutch
His fate was that he fell to his knees
For all he had to eat were sweets day and night
And he gave everyone such a fright
So now he knows to try to eat some wheat and meat.

Harry Peter Dibben (9)
Maldon Court Preparatory School, Maldon

My Brother

M y brother is so messy! He chucks his socks
everywhere!
Y ou better get them in the wash or the house will
be smelly!

B ig brother why do you eat tons of chocolate?
R oom is so messy, there are wrappers
everywhere!
O h your room needs a big clean by a professional
cleaner
T o your surprise not even a cleaner will go in
there!
H e is so lazy I wish he would have a shower
E ven if he was clean for half an hour
R eally you need to have healthy food like a
banana, big brother.

Max Muson (7)
Maldon Court Preparatory School, Maldon

Winter

As the snowflakes drizzled downwards
Eagles and blackbirds rose upwards
The deer scampered though the woods quite slow
And tall trees got pounded with snow.

The lake like a road made of an ice sheet
The golden sun is trying to heat
The freezing cold animals feeding
Whilst their feet are scratched and bleeding.

Cold biting at everything in sight
The garden of snow was bright
As snow lay motionless on the ground
The moles had piled earth into a mound.

Toby Wilson (10)
Maldon Court Preparatory School, Maldon

Minecraft

M ine, mine mine, my pickaxe has broken oh no
I'm stuck
I 'm being chased by creepers and I need to run
fast
N o, argh I'm dead
E r, what just happened, I died again
C reative is my favourite, I can't die and I got a
stack of diamonds
R eally it is my favourite game, it is just so cool
A nvils are cool because you can enchant and
even rename
F ond of it you should be
T hanks for releasing 1.15!

Freddy Bruce (7)
Maldon Court Preparatory School, Maldon

Embarrassed

Yesterday I did bad things
I'm sorry for smashing your brand new TV
I would pay for it, but we needed a brand new one anyway
I'm sorry for trapping your sister in the dark,
But actually I quite enjoyed the peace and quiet
I'm a very sorry child but actually I'm not sorry
Because the TV was too old-fashioned
And your sister was way too annoying and so smelly
So I'm not sorry for anything and it's quite your fault!

Jacob Tsai (8)
Maldon Court Preparatory School, Maldon

My Brother

M y brother is a lolly sucker
Y es he is a pain

B ut he has a banana brain
R eally happy when he has his scrunchy teddy
O h but he is unhappy when the teddy is not there
T he only way to stop him screaming is with a lolly
H e is a diva
E ven if my parents don't believe that
R ight now he is playing in his room and I can hear him smashing something right now.

Jacob Day (7)
Maldon Court Preparatory School, Maldon

Zane's Cautionary Tale

There once was a boy named Zane
Who would go into pain
When he had to do bothersome studies
He would rather play Call of Duty
His mum was so worried
He was quickly scurried
To the messy Chelmsford A&E
He was in odious agony
He suddenly found a laser gun
Now he was going to be done
As he lay in the hospital bed
He picked up the gun and *bang!*
He was dead.

Aden Karimi (10)
Maldon Court Preparatory School, Maldon

The Forest

Forest, forest, forest,
Twisting, turning, intertwining,
Trunks weaving in-between the others like a race

Forest, forest, forest,
Towering, covering, tall
Showing no consent for the sun to come through

Forest, forest, forest,
Magical, mythical, adventurous
People flabbergasted as the tall wooden soldiers cover them from above.

Benjamin Philips (10)
Maldon Court Preparatory School, Maldon

Purple

Purple looks like a whole new galaxy
Purple smells like freshly picked grapes, they explode with juice
Purple tastes like mystery of the most powerful stars in the sky
Purple sounds like a million whispers coming to you at once
Purple feels like you are touching he fluffiest pillow in the world
Purple makes me feel like I am in a different world.

Vincent Arthur Lower (7)
Maldon Court Preparatory School, Maldon

I'm Not Sorry

One day I was playing an intense alien game
And the aliens were about to invade
The only way to save myself
Was to paint my plain as white paper rocket green
Green blinds aliens because it's the colour of broccoli
It almost blinded me too
I'm sorry for painting your plain white walls green
But they were a bit boring before.

India Fisher (8)
Maldon Court Preparatory School, Maldon

Mitch, Who Was Addicted To Mario Kart

There once was a boy named Mitch
Who was addicted to his Nintendo Switch
As he played Mario Kart
He let out a great fart
It led to such a dreadful fate
The story I shall now relate
Poor Mitch in inhaled the dreadful smell
As soon as he smelt it he fell
The poor boy is now outdated
You guessed it, Mitch suffocated!

Miguel Mandla Businge Kitasoboka (10)
Maldon Court Preparatory School, Maldon

The Witching Hour

In the middle of the night
By the full moon's light
Monsters come out at the dead of night

Witches with hats
Broomsticks and cats
Walking along swiftly

Skeletons, ghosts
Standing by posts
Watching the scene go by

But in the houses
As quiet as mouses
The people still sleep.

Alice Wilson (9)
Maldon Court Preparatory School, Maldon

My Alien

One day during our school play
No one was allowed to say
What happened the other day.

The other day an alien came
Riding on an aeroplane
His name was Betsy
And his wife was named Lexi.

He asked to stay
But he didn't pay
Then it was time to say goodbye
And I ate a space pie.

Arnold Head (9)
Maldon Court Preparatory School, Maldon

Why Do I Have A Sibling?

B ruder toys, he has so many
R unning around, he never stops
O ther brothers just can't compare
T eamwork is his best thing
H e gives the best hugs
E veryone is his friend
R ed is the colour for love
Why do I have a sibling? I want TWO siblings!

Anna Barnett (7)
Maldon Court Preparatory School, Maldon

What If...

What if my mum
Fought off intergalactic aliens from Mars
Auditioned in the X Factor as a soloist
Won the Great British Bake Off with a blindfold on
Flew to Jupiter and back, dragging along Dad
Bought a baby manatee as a pet for me
Somehow managed to teach the school
And made it back for tea!

Sophie Clark (10)
Maldon Court Preparatory School, Maldon

I Am Sorry

I broke the door because it was in my way
Someone locked the door
I am very sorry for destroying it
But I just wanted my trike
I am sorry for taking my brother's toys
But he was just being a menace and making a noise
If you want me to do my homework
I need some peace and quiet so shh...

Harry Barker (7)
Maldon Court Preparatory School, Maldon

Kittens

K ittens love to drink milk
I n the garden kittens play in the long garden
T en lovely cuddles a day
T hey are cute and very cuddly
E ating cat food twice a day
N ot always friendly when they bite
S ometimes smelly but always cute.

Darcy Ephrave (8)
Maldon Court Preparatory School, Maldon

Baby Pink

Baby pink looks like a warm hug on a cold winter's day
Baby pink smells like fresh and juicy lemonade
Baby pink tastes like a delicious yummy doughnut with thousands of sprinkles on top
Baby pink sounds like a newborn baby being born
Baby pink feels like some delicious stew.

Lauren Griggs (7)
Maldon Court Preparatory School, Maldon

The Seaside

S unny seaside!
E ating ice cream is yummy
A mazing sandcastles are the best
S unday fun!
I can see a crab
D addy is coming in the sea with us
E ating fish and chips is very nice.

Jack Gower (9)
Maldon Court Preparatory School, Maldon

Football

F antastic football skills
O utstanding
O ptimistic
T hrilling
B all everywhere on the pitch
A lways keep your head up
L eadership
L oyalty.

Jake Rainger (8)
Maldon Court Preparatory School, Maldon

Hockey

H aving fun, scoring goals
O pposition ready to play
C reating space on the pitch
K nocking balls off the pitch
E asy game with under 8s
Y es! We won.

Harry Mason (9)
Maldon Court Preparatory School, Maldon

Dance

D ance is so beautiful
A nd lovely to watch
N ice and relaxing
C ute when tiny children do it
E asy to learn, just take one step.

Kitty Ross (9)
Maldon Court Preparatory School, Maldon

The Solar System

Jumping Jupiter ready to break the galaxy
Magnificent Mars as red as flames ready to spread
Spectacular Saturn ready to be the leader
Nerdy Neptune glancing at the galaxy
Excellent Earth made liveable for humans
Violent Venus ready to kill the others
Outstanding Uranus waiting to be the greatest
Scolding sun ready to scorch.

Sophie Howorth (10)
Maldon Primary School, Maldon

The Death Of War

The rain falls like popcorn coming out the sky
The mud squelches through soldiers' boots
The rats and mice skip all around the battlefield
And some of them even die by the shots from the men
And some of the men itch because the lice creep up on them
In the silence a mournful owl hoots
The noise, the silence, the rain
And the squelchy mud
And for some people it's all too much
The scream of bombs exploding
As soldiers land with a thud
If only this were a dream
I don't want this disgraceful and disastrous war
To happen to any of you people
Our enemy will be our friend
So we will never ever have war ever again
So the world will not get damaged
So you can walk everywhere you go
To get food, clothes, and everything you need.

Sheja Dylan Kananura (9)
Our Lady's Catholic Primary School, Cowley

Soldiers

They camp in the trenches with their eyes open like an owl
One of the soldiers shouts, "Enemy!" *Boom!*
The sandbags and the barbed wire fell
The soldiers stamped to the enemy's camp
Destroying everything in their path
They race rapidly, raging across the battlefield
Some get shot and scream in pain
Some of the soldiers sacrifice themselves to save other soldiers
Most fear that the war will never end
On their way back to the trenches they hear guns firing
Bang! But they ignore them
They walk to the trenches with mud oozing through their boots
Some men march back to the rock-solid trenches
With blood dripping down their faces and arms
While others walk blind, so need help
Getting across the death trap of war
To get to the dark trenches

Bang! Bang! Bang!
Planes in the sky
Are fighting above the trenches
Men march making not one sound
Many men come back dead with people carrying them
"Oh when will this war end?" a soldier says
But they do not lose hope
They stay happy and hope this war will end
The soldiers go up to the battlefield to fight again
But most soldiers die by being sacrificed
The glittering sky turns as black as night
The great big pond gets smaller each dying second
Everything is blood
Rain drips, thunder in the clouds
One struck by lightning
Soldiers cover their hearts
Bang! The shots still go
A few months later the soldiers hear some singing
"It is Christmas," shouts a soldier giggling and jumping around
But that doesn't last for long

Soldiers sob, screaming and frozen in fear
Some go crazy, some run out of the trenches and get shot
Frostbite covers their arms
Sickness passes around
Dirt gets in their eyes
The sun blinds their eyes
But do they give up?
Some of them die but the rest
Oh they stay strong, very strong
One of the soldiers makes a speech about not giving up
He says, "What would your wife think? Who are you?
You joined the army!"
But no one listens
All of the soldiers start praying to the Lord God
Because everyone has lost hope
This war will never end
Soldiers scream, stampede in fear and disappointment

Some soldiers are allowed to leave early but others aren't
They are alone, missing their family
A few years later, the war ends
They all go back
And pray for all those who sacrificed themselves to save us
And for the people who died.

Marvin Da Silva (9)
Our Lady's Catholic Primary School, Cowley

What Do Planets Say

I'm the sun, the biggest thing
Can't you see,
Centre of the solar system
All the planets go around me,

I'm so hot
So let's go to the planet closest to me

I'm Mercury,
The smallest planet
I always spin so slow

I'm Venus,
I've got volcanos
That say hey ho,
I'm the same size as Earth
But spin the other way

I'm Earth,
I'm such a beautiful world
Home to all the boys and girls

I'm Mars, the red planet
I have no ice
But two moons,
That's quite nice

I'm Jupiter,
I'm so big,
I spin the fastest and I'm handsome

I'm Saturn,
I've got rings made of rocks and other things

I'm Uranus,
I say that with pride
No I lied, I'm lying on my side

I'm Neptune,
Windy and serious
Bring an umbrella I'm so serious.

Lamari Sackey-Nash (11)
Our Lady's Catholic Primary School, Cowley

Soldiers

Soldiers in war on a dangerous battleground
Fire! Fire! Fire! They are instructed
Pistols are cracking
The smoke is rising
The sky is dark and dim
Attack!
Launch!
Attack!
Ceasefire
Soldiers take cover
Soldiers in war bombarded
A *crash, boom, bang!*
A bloody wounded soldier seen crawling back to base
"This war is living hell!" he cries
Soldiers with weapons creep forward
And crouch with troops that follow behind
A soldier of war found wounded and down
Limbs blown off
Screams and cries of terror and pain
Can be heard far and wide

That soldier of war is sadly no more
May he rest in peace
The fight for freedom is over for him
But he does not die in vain
Our country will be liberated
And we'll remember his good name.

Thomas Cassitta (8)
Our Lady's Catholic Primary School, Cowley

Out Of This World

A person called Mr Box went to the rocket
He went to space
He went to the moon
He jumped up and up until he saw aliens
One was a teacher and five children
Learning about being crazy
The aliens saw him, he ran to the rocket
He flew to the space station
Mr Box saw a red button
He pressed the button
A voice said, "In ten seconds the space station will blow."
Mr Box went to the rocket and went back to Earth
People on Earth saw a dot coming from space
It hit the water so hard
Ed and Ems went to the rocket
The news on Channel 6 said
A person came from the rocket called Mr Box
He said to the TV, "I saw aliens!"

Bartosz Bok (10)
Our Lady's Catholic Primary School, Cowley

The Crazy War Game

Once the cloudy fog coming down
From the sky like a tornado
And everyone heard shells banging in town
There was a battle going on
All of the soldiers heard it from miles away
The plane was huge like a house
The plane crashed into France
In the battlefield all the soldiers' boots were oozing
The bombs were booming everywhere
All of the horses died during the war
It was incredibly insane
All of the horses were hungry, they were poor
The German army were attacking the British
And their tanks going *boom bam bash*
The bombs were falling from the sky
But they were safe in the trenches.

Henna Singh (8)
Our Lady's Catholic Primary School, Cowley

This Is The War

They died for us
The fought for us
Just for this life
It's more than a stabbing knife
This is the war
This is the war
Countries mourning for peace day and night
This is the war
This is the war
How could they bear this sight?
The woman panting for her breath
When she found out about her husband's death
This is the war
This is the war
Oh how he ran
This is the war
This is the war
Just to save that man
As we remember them
How they held the pain
And they didn't do it in vain

So let's spread the peace for those men
This is the war
This is the war.

Annabelle Thomas (8)
Our Lady's Catholic Primary School, Cowley

World War One

I was dusty like a basement
Every second someone will hide somewhere
No one will know where they are
The people will run out of bullets
And will have no more bullets left
The people die in seconds because the rocks trip them over like crazy
The people run around looking
Looking for their partners
When the bullets go through their heads
The people have tapes in their backpacks
Flying around and killing people
Tanks are moving like slow dangerous men
The women hide behind the men
And the men get shot
World War One, people go in the tanks
And they don't know what they're shooting at.

Aaliyah Galloway (9)
Our Lady's Catholic Primary School, Cowley

The Never Stopping War

The old bells sadly drop, *bang!*
The sky is getting dark
The rain falls like midnight moons
The mud oozes out from my boots
The cold starry night
The squeak of rats
The itch of lice
The boom of shells
The noise
The mournful
Me as the poor soldier
Boom, boom, boom went the tanks
The enemy is already training
The owls are hooting
The women screaming
I never felt so separated from my family
It's so gross because the war is just a dorky stinky place
With no food
I'm getting way too weak
That's why I'm starting to die.

Giulia Dos (9)
Our Lady's Catholic Primary School, Cowley

The War Of Doom

In the battlefield of death
Everybody had their last breath
Guns spitting out rapid shots
Filling people with blood-filled dots
All we could see was a massive fire
The painful future was looking dire
Everywhere there are bodies burning
Flames go up, twisting, turning

Tanks moved like slow, secretive men
Blowing soldiers up at quarter to ten
Submarines swim under the land
Giving the soldiers a much needed helping hand
Missions happening secretly
In the ocean is where we'll be
Bumps are chilling in the sky
Protecting soldiers so they don't die.

Blake O'Brien (9)
Our Lady's Catholic Primary School, Cowley

War

One day two boys were playing a game of WWI.
They built two long holes in the mud
They brought two ladders and said
"We made our trenches."
When it was dinnertime
The boys pretended to come home from the war.

Then the boys had grown up
And they found their hats from when they were little
They said, "We should go to war."

My great uncle Cyril was on a battleship in WWII
It probably smelt like seawater
And probably his shipmates smelt too
He might have smelt gas or smoke
And probably rat poo and wee.

Areya Kerr-Wakeham (9)
Our Lady's Catholic Primary School, Cowley

The Gods

Jupiter the one of all
Who roams the world
Head of all with his wife Juno
Who doesn't know the awe

Here comes Mars
The Roman god of war
That comes with a chariot
With blood and gore

Neptune, Poseidon,
Second best of 'em all
But comes blue and cold

Vulcan bang crash
In his forges
With metal and silver and gold.

Last but not least
Golden boy
Apollo, Greek mythology
Zeus and Leto raise him

Poetry, music and healing
Gifted the dice for which Venus
After his cattle was in treason.

Danyl Stephen (10)
Our Lady's Catholic Primary School, Cowley

War Poem

The people's shoes disappear
And the water isn't very clear
They still have to fight
In the darkness
Without light or peace
Germans run while the British fire their guns
Soldiers write letters while war birds pick their feathers
Maybe some day they could end war

I don't think people with that much fear in their eyes
Would be blinking any more
We don't have to worry any more though
Because war is no more
This I know
I know what you're thinking
There might be World War three
But not, hopefully.

Eva Barrett (8)
Our Lady's Catholic Primary School, Cowley

In The War

Boom, boom! Bombs everywhere, *kaboom!*
There are bombs for sure
Smash! That was the enemy
Bang, bang, boom! Big bombs everywhere.

Do I have to say at the front line?
A person just died, the rain is too heavy
There are planes in the sky. We need tanks.
It is raining too heavy for aeroplanes.

My boots are filling up with water
All I can hear is *squelch*.
Everybody get behind a tree, otherwise we will get shot
Boom, boom, kaboom! C'mon, let's go fighting.

Jayden Adams (8)
Our Lady's Catholic Primary School, Cowley

War Never Ends

I'm waiting for him to come back
Is he dead or is he alive?
Life here is like a sack
I'm waiting for him with a piece of pie
Because war never ends.

Will those high heroes ever come here
Or is it too late and I am a weeping widow?
He knew how to use those gears
Because he is the greatest foe
And war never ends.

War isn't you fighting for glory
All you do is arrive from a ship
Then ends as a gloomy story
Some people say it's just a fib
Because war never ends.

Anas Awais (8)
Our Lady's Catholic Primary School, Cowley

Justice League

A world with a speedster
You would see him in a flash.
A world with a Kryptonian
He is powered by the sun.
Cyborg has a pet name Cory
He is powered by an alien source.
He dresses like a bat
The Dark Knight gives crime fear
He gets a knife, scrapes the car.
He has a ring powered by a lantern,
Enemy the Yellow Lantern
The opposite of will is fear
Green and yellow.
The Amazon
She has iron things to block electricity.
The give criminals fear
Beware, the Justice League is here.

Jayden Munyampundu (9)
Our Lady's Catholic Primary School, Cowley

The Great War

As the rain spatters down from the sky
The soldiers climb out of the rat-infested trenches
It is here where violence is found
With the boom of the shells and the men
stumbling, bleeding, injured
Hundreds of men that have lost their lives
Are lying in heaps as the earth sheds a tear for
them
The beloved ones at home
Wistful wives and cheerful children
Weep when they get the terrible news
And now, they will rest calmly, silently
As they rest in the fields
Where the poppies grow.

India Rose Zinyama (8)
Our Lady's Catholic Primary School, Cowley

My Favourite Thing

My favourite thing is slime
It's great to poke and stretch
Sometimes it can be a bit messy
So you should keep it in the pot
My favourite thing is slime

The galaxy is some people's favourite colour
It's good in slime, in cake
I like it in animals.

My favourite food is chocolate
It's creamy and delicious
Full of sugar
No one can top it
Because chocolate is delicious
My favourite food is chocolate.

Iona Murphy-Spiers (10)
Our Lady's Catholic Primary School, Cowley

The Candy Shop On The Moon

When I hop on the moon
I straight away jump to the candy shop
I ask Mum if I can buy
Candy from the shop
She says no
Outside the candy shop
I find a coin on the candy floor
Outside the candy shop
There are lots to choose from
At last I choose the lollipop
It's bigger than my face
And it's super yum
I give my brother one lick
But no more
This poem's about
The candy shop on the moon.

Rand Alsahli (11)
Our Lady's Catholic Primary School, Cowley

War Days

I fight on the battlefield, old and big
Surrounded by soldiers dead on the battlefield
Screaming bombs around me
I carry my gun with me
Bang! Boom!
The bombs cry around me.
When we are in the trenches we stay
uncomfortable
Mud is oozing through our boots
Most people are mad and they try to shoot me
I try to shoot my enemy
Some people around me do it just for fun
But for some it's really scary.

Chloe Lobo (9)
Our Lady's Catholic Primary School, Cowley

Sunny Days

In the beach where the sand flows
In the beach where the wind blows
With a blow of the wind
It whizzed through the long blue sea

Some sleep, some dance and some play
But nobody wants to lie
Some hide, but most want to leap
Some seek, some want to stay, but they sleep

Chirping birds high in the sky
Some play, some lie, but birds fly
Some birds broke their wings so they cry.

Blossom Vas (7)
Our Lady's Catholic Primary School, Cowley

Space Ball

As the stars form into a goal
I leap from star to star to score
As I cheer and leap
The stars give me a little twinkle
As I see the alien without hair
Giving me a glare
Ronald giving me a smile
The other team frowning
Whilst we're cheering
We shake hands after the match
And give a little smile
Then the stars rain down
Like glitter and rain.

Tavonga Mutsenhure (10)
Our Lady's Catholic Primary School, Cowley

Remembrance Time

On the battlefield old and ruined
The dead are there battered and new
Squelching through the dirt and mud
Those stupid silly generals posh and scared
They don't even know how dreadful they are
The guns go *ping* and the bombs go *boom*
The rain comes thumping down like thunder
So poor they are in the dreadful war
The darkness sucks them in.

Barra Baseby (8)
Our Lady's Catholic Primary School, Cowley

The Living

War for all the living is done
Wounded soldiers is what we had
Lots of people did it for fun
Also carrying a great big gun
Most people were very mad
For the living good and bad
Bang! Horrific days in the dark

Larks bravely singing fly
High in the sky
Silver church bells
Instead of jail cells
For the living
Is the One!

Florence Riley (8)
Our Lady's Catholic Primary School, Cowley

Planes

The soldiers tried to be brave
But they got stuck and could not save
The planes would fly
Really really high
Some lay in dirt
And some were a little bit hurt
The people in the plane would fly
And the ones down below would die
The planes will take flight in the night
We remember the month before December.

Gemma Teffe (8)
Our Lady's Catholic Primary School, Cowley

The World War

The bomb was thrown
And then it flew and flew as it grew
When the bomb exploded they shot with fright
Now it's evening we need to fight
Lots of people died
As they ran for help with one last breath
As they ran they fell into death
For Franz Ferdinand we fight and fight
As it makes a fright.

Astou Diop (9)
Our Lady's Catholic Primary School, Cowley

War Poem

In the middle of the night, the rain falls like bells
The mud smooshes through my boots
Our loved ones hide from the war
We will come again
We shall carry on the war
And never give up
This night will never be quiet again
This night will never shine bright again
It will affect the world.

Lukas Rimsa (8)
Our Lady's Catholic Primary School, Cowley

The Fight In World War One

The soldiers would fight
All through the night
They shoot their gun
All through the sun
They keep their breath
Before their death
They keep down low
In the snow
They are really brave
When they hear someone they run into a cave
When they lose they are sad
And really mad.

Tallulah Carter (8)
Our Lady's Catholic Primary School, Cowley

In The Future

I don't think we are going to survive
Our planet is turning to ashes in a second
Ask California, they will tell you about it
Don't come to me when your fur coat isn't clean
Don't come to me when your child can't think
When tigers became extinct
In the future.

Abigail Alex (10)
Our Lady's Catholic Primary School, Cowley

War

World War One where soldiers and animals die
It's all sad and scary, we must stop the war
It's so so horrible
It's the worst war ever
If the war stops the soldiers and enemies will be friends
Everybody out walking for fresh air
Training for the war outside.

Mia Cisneros Jordan (7)
Our Lady's Catholic Primary School, Cowley

Out Of This World

You are my favourite thing
You are the stars of the night
You are with me wherever I go
You are the galaxy of the world
The blue sky is everywhere
You are the Roman gods of the sky
There are black holes wherever you go
Plants are everywhere and they will stay.

Evelyn Denton (11)
Our Lady's Catholic Primary School, Cowley

The Long Lasting War

Nearly every day we are covered in blood
Our boots are always filled with mud
We never get the lovely peace
It always goes to an increase
When we sleep we hear bells
But when we are awake we hear shells
A lot of men cry and cry
But a lot of men die and die.

Leila Kent (9)
Our Lady's Catholic Primary School, Cowley

Courage

The thunder rains like a flood
But doesn't stop the fight
If a blizzard comes and they get frostbite
They still do not give up
If the sun is hot and they get burnt
They carry on
The snow melts like boiling water is poured on it
They keep fighting.

Daniel Vasnevicius (9)
Our Lady's Catholic Primary School, Cowley

Space Candy

Yum yum yum
Lovely space candy
You make me happy
With cheers and laughter
When I skip to the candy shop
You make me hungry
For more candy
With rainbows and moons
With people and you
I love you candy
And I always will.

Amy Renny (11)
Our Lady's Catholic Primary School, Cowley

War Poem

The rain at night dripping gently
Splish splash
Sleeping in my bed comfy and relaxing
I put my coat on and my shoes
Outside the mud oozes in my shoes
I see colourful fireworks
Boom
I run and hide.

Pritika Kumar (8)
Our Lady's Catholic Primary School, Cowley

The War

Out of the window I saw war
I ran downstairs and hit the back door
So I swore
My sister heard me so I did a roar
I heard a shot
My friend was rot
I started to cry
So I looked to the sky
And started to fly.

Olamide Olagundoye (10)
Our Lady's Catholic Primary School, Cowley

War

The gunshots were loud and they went *pow!*
The bombs went *boom* and the soldiers ran
But the Russians laughed and attacked
Everyone ran and they went ha ha ha
The bombs went *bang* and they never slept.

Kayden Dikokoble (7)
Our Lady's Catholic Primary School, Cowley

Homework

Homework, always harsh
Giving me spellings day and night
Keeping me awake
What will my teacher say?
Will he shout or will he not
I wonder what he will say
I'm too scared about what he will say.

Aina Grisales (9)
Our Lady's Catholic Primary School, Cowley

The Pain Of War

After the war, one of the soldiers that survived
Told his son how painful it was
The rain was dropping like lightning
Noise like 1000 cars driving
It was painful, like fifty cars driving over you.

Gabriel Prigodski (7)
Our Lady's Catholic Primary School, Cowley

In Flanders Fields

In Flanders Fields
Where all is quiet
The poppies grow in peace
No shouting or any bombs going boom!
Had no rooms, they had to sleep in the trenches
Where it was muddy and squelchy.

Jamie Mason (9)
Our Lady's Catholic Primary School, Cowley

The War Tour

I am going to give you a tour of the war fields
Look at the bomb and the guns gone
Can you see the tanks and horses and planes?
Look at the soldiers and pets
Boom! Boom!

Kaiti Farruku (8)
Our Lady's Catholic Primary School, Cowley

The Magpie

The magpie likes to steal
They like shiny things
The ring
The tin
The shiny bin
Is the shiniest of them all.

Marcin Lasocha (11)
Our Lady's Catholic Primary School, Cowley

Dream Worlds

Dreams soar
Some roar
And some adore
Others cry
While others fly
Above the rest
Dreams are the best!

Riley Davies (11)
Our Lady's Catholic Primary School, Cowley

Meeting The Knowledge Giver

I met a talented and elegant Knowledge Giver
She was as wise as an owl
Her smile was as bright as the beaming sun
She wore a shimmering dark blue dress with a magical and heart-shaped necklace
I followed the intelligent Knowledge Giver
She flew like a swan
She was as fast as sound
She moved like a secret agent
She was as cunning as a fox
The Knowledge Giver softly floated down into the poshest school in town
The Knowledge Giver paused at the filthy edge of the classroom
It was as quiet as space
It was as still as a statue
Suddenly she spotted someone struggling with a maths equation
In a blink of an eye she vanished
Who was she about to give knowledge to?

Gabriella Ekole (8)
St Alfege With St Peter's CE Primary School, Greenwich

Meeting The Knowledge Giver

I met the Knowledge Giver
He was as bright as God's angels
His smile was as bright as a diamond
He wore a Norwegian dress with a light rainbow cape

I followed him
He flew like a unicorn secret agent
He moved like a flying cheetah who could collect sound
He made a knowledge bubble and lightly floated down into Neverland
The Knowledge Giver paused at the edge of Neverland
It was as busy as New York City it was as noisy as a circus and a funfair combined
I heard Peter Pan fighting Captain Hook
And Wendy locked with the Lost Boys

Suddenly he heard someone doing a test in the distance
In a blink of an eye he disappeared
Whose knowledge power was he about to give?

Israel Oke (8)
St Alfege With St Peter's CE Primary School, Greenwich

Meeting The Knowledge Giver

I met the Knowledge Giver
He was as fiery as a crackling flame
His smile was as vivid as a diamond
He wore a light blue T-shirt and crimson shorts
With a watermelon on it

I followed him
He flew like a bald eagle
He moved like an undercover man
He flew to Phoenix, Arizona
The Knowledge Giver paused at the edge of the country
It was as busy as New York
It was as big as the world
Suddenly he saw a child struggling to read
In a blink of an eye he faded away
Where was he going?
The next day I saw the anger thief
He was amazing.

Tareyah Hancel (8)
St Alfege With St Peter's CE Primary School, Greenwich

Meeting The Tooth Fairy

I met the tooth fairy
She was as beautiful as a model
Her smile was as bright as the sun
She wore a light red dress with brown boots

I followed her
She flew like an aeroplane
She moved like a secret agent
She floated down into Fairyland

The tooth fairy suddenly paused at the edge of Fairyland
It was as gorgeous as seeing an enchanted forest
It was as silent as a statue
Suddenly the tooth fairy heard screaming in the distance
In the blink of an eye she vanished
Whos tooth was going to be exchanged with a coin?

Hannah Adetayo-Eyesigha (8)
St Alfege With St Peter's CE Primary School, Greenwich

Meeting The Anger Thief

I met the anger thief
He was as thrilled as an enthusiastic fish
His eyes were as sparkly as diamonds
He wore a vivid orange jumper with a
multicoloured bracelet

I followed him
He swooped as fast as an eagle
He moved like a snake
He glided down to a football stadium

The anger thief froze at the edge of the stadium
It was as quiet as a mouse eating cheese
It was as still as a tree
Suddenly he heard someone shouting in the
distance
In the blink of an eye he vanished
Whose anger gems was he about to take?

Joseph Sukte (8)
St Alfege With St Peter's CE Primary School, Greenwich

Meeting The Worry Thief

I met the worries thief
She was as cute as a stunning puppy
Her smile was as dazzling as a star
She wore a cool rainbow dress with a lovely jumper

I followed her harmlessly
She glided like a pigeon
She moved like a llama galloping
She floated down into a school speedily
She froze at the edge
It was as calm as a baby watching TV

It was as still as darkness
Suddenly she heard worries in the distance
In the blink of an eye she faded
Whose worries was she going to take without permission?

Sharon Adetayo-Eyesigha (8)
St Alfege With St Peter's CE Primary School, Greenwich

Meeting The Knowledge Giver King

I met the knowledge giver king
He was as stunning as a king
His smile was as bright as a sunflower
I followed him
He fluttered like a butterfly
He moved like a spy

He flew down to Disneyland
It was so loud like the cartoon of the loud house
It was as loud as a gorilla
Suddenly he heard a boy crying in the distance
The little boy couldn't read because he's blind
So he gave him knowledge
In a blink of an eye he vanished
Whose knowledge will he give to people next?

Gabriella Pereira (7)
St Alfege With St Peter's CE Primary School, Greenwich

Meeting The Book Reader

I met the book reader
He was as happy as winning a book competition
He was as cool as a rock star
His smile was as bright as gold

He wore cool glasses with a red watermelon jumper
I followed him
He flew like a plane
He moved like a spy

He ended on top of St Alfege school
He paused at the end of the village
It was as quiet as a basement
It was as still as a statue
Suddenly he saw someone struggling to read
In a blink he vanished
Whose book did he read?

Mateo Garcia (8)
St Alfege With St Peter's CE Primary School, Greenwich

Meeting The Tooth Fairy

I met a tooth fairy
He is pretty like angels
His slime is bright like ice
He wears a tooth fairy suit with a tooth fairy necklace

I follow him
He flies like an aeroplane
He moves like a ninja
He floats down to England

He pauses on the edge of England
It is quiet like light
It is as still as a house
Suddenly he hears someone with a painful tooth
Crying out in pain
In the blink of an eye
He vanishes
Whose tooth is he going to take?

Rani Saleh (8)
St Alfege With St Peter's CE Primary School, Greenwich

Meeting The Angry Thief

I met the angry thief
He is as angry as a bull
He is as strong as a panther
He has a costume with three colours

I followed him
He flew like pepper
He moved like a ninja
He flew to a football match

The angry thief paused in the middle of the
football match
It was as loud as a bomb
It was as happy as a disco
Suddenly I hear someone angry

In one blink of an eye the angry thief vanishes
Whose anger is he going to take?

Jayden Igbanu (8)
St Alfege With St Peter's CE Primary School, Greenwich

Meeting The Knowledge Giver

I met the knowledge giver
She was as happy as a sunflower
Her lips were as bright as diamonds
She wore a light yellow dress with a diamond necklace

I followed her
She flew like an owl
She moved like a butterfly
She floated down to a pool
She stopped at the edge of the pool
It was as quiet as a mouse
It was as still as a tree
Suddenly she heard someone crying in the house
In a blink of an eye she vanished
Where was she going?

Lauren Copeland (8)
St Alfege With St Peter's CE Primary School, Greenwich

Meeting The Happy Giver

I met the happy giver
She was as striking as a sunflower
Her smile was as bright as a lightbulb
She wore a dark red jumper with light blue joggers and a ring

I followed her
She ran like a cheetah
She moved like a spy
She ran to a school
She paused at the school edge

It was as quiet as darkness
It was as still as a statue
Suddenly she heard someone shouting
In a blink of an eye she vanished
Who was she going to help?

Saya Tran (8)
St Alfege With St Peter's CE Primary School, Greenwich

Meeting The Hug Giver

I met the hug giver
She was as big as a lamp post
She wore a pink T-shirt with a rough trouser

I followed her
She flew like a brisk kite
She moved like a Stone Age person
She floated down to a stunning hill

She paused at the hill edge
It was as loud as children playing in the park
It was as still as a striking statue
Suddenly she heard a louder voice
In a blink of an eye she vanished
What voice did she hear?

Christine Nakazibwe (8)
St Alfege With St Peter's CE Primary School, Greenwich

Meeting The Happy Giver

I met the happy giver,
She was as busy as a bee.
Her smile was as bright as a diamond.
She wore a light pink dress with a necklace
I followed her.
She was as fast as a cheetah.
She moved like a duck,
She floated to a lake.
She paused at the edge of the lake,
It was quiet like space.
Suddenly, she saw a boy crying in the distance.
In a blink of an eye, she vanished.
Who does the happy giver need to give happiness to next?

Shanice Fosu (7)
St Alfege With St Peter's CE Primary School, Greenwich

The Story Of The Knowledge Giver

I met the Knowledge Giver
She was as pretty as a butterfly
Her eyes were as bright as a candle
She wore a light pink strawberry dress
With a cloud and sun necklace

I followed her
She flew like a crane
She moved like a snake
She floated to Disneyland

She paused at the edge of Disneyland
It was as loud as fireworks
As still as a tree
Suddenly she saw a book
In a blink of an eye she vanished.

Aishani Louison-Davis (8)
St Alfege With St Peter's CE Primary School, Greenwich

Meeting The Sadness Thief

I met the sadness thief
She was as quiet as darkness
Her smile was as bright as diamonds
She wore a light blue dress with a pearl necklace

I followed her
She flew like a butterfly
She moved like a spy
She floated down to a forest
She froze by the edge of the forest
Suddenly she heard crying
It was as loud as a football team that won
She sped away
Whose tears was she about to stop?

Deborah Sunday (7)
St Alfege With St Peter's CE Primary School, Greenwich

Meeting The Angry Thief

I met the angry thief
He was as quiet as darkness
His smile was as bright as a diamond
I followed him
He flew like a rapid plane
He was as brisk as a cheetah
He floated to a magical football match
Then he paused at the edge of a school
It was as quiet as paper
It was as busy as God
Then he saw someone furious
In the blink of an eye he vanished
Whose angriness was he about to take?

Eden Anobili (7)
St Alfege With St Peter's CE Primary School, Greenwich

The Worry Thief

I met the worry thief
He was as stripy as a zebra
His smile was as bright as the sun
He wore an orange and green stripy shirt
With a clover on it
He flew like a plane
He moved like a spy
He stopped at the edge of the village
He was as quiet as a turtle
Suddenly I heard worries
In a blink of an eye it vanished
Whose worry did he take?

Sina Ashouri (8)
St Alfege With St Peter's CE Primary School, Greenwich

The Worry Thief

I met the worry thief
He was as pretty as a firework
His smile was as bright as a ruby
He wore a spysuit
I followed him
I flew like a blackbird
He moved like a ninja
He floated down to the city

He paused at the edge of the city
It was as still as a house
Suddenly from the distance I heard crying
When is he coming back?

Bessem Kececi (8)
St Alfege With St Peter's CE Primary School, Greenwich

Happy Giver

I met the happy giver
He's as cool as a rockstar
His smile is as bright as a diamond
He wore a yellow shirt with a magnificent tail
He runs like a cheetah and walks like a lion
catching his prey
The happy giver went to a cool football match
He heard crying in the distance
Who was the happy giver going to make happy
again?

Weigle (7)
St Alfege With St Peter's CE Primary School, Greenwich

Meeting The Book Thief

I met the book thief
She was as pretty as a butterfly
Her smile was as bright as a diamond
She wore a mask with a pearl necklace
I followed her
She flew like a bird
She moved like a ninja
She floated down to a village
I paused at the edge of a village
It was quiet.

Flourish Bamidele (7)
St Alfege With St Peter's CE Primary School, Greenwich

Miss Oliver

There was a girl called Miss Oliver
Her hair was long like Rapunzel
Her dress was as fluffy as a bunny
Her earrings were as shiny as a ring
Her mouth was as big as a small clock
Her dress was sparkly as a bird
Her hair was as black as a mouse.

Charlie Quickenden (7)
St Alfege With St Peter's CE Primary School, Greenwich

Meeting The Worry Thief

I met the worry thief
He was as pretty as a cat
His smile was as bright as a sun
He wore a skeleton suit
He flew like an eagle
He moved like a ninja
He floated in a cave.

Ryan Bui (7)
St Alfege With St Peter's CE Primary School, Greenwich

The Tear Thief

The tear thief is nice
The tear thief is good
The tear thief is happy

Cherik Mafolo-Bitsindou (7)
St Alfege With St Peter's CE Primary School, Greenwich

Space Exploration

S pace is the best place to be
P acing around with me
A nd maybe even land on the moon
C an't we go home soon?
E xtra-terrestrial on Planet Mars

E mily, can I have one of those space bars?
X is for extra-terrestrial (I know it doesn't start with X)
P rancing and dancing on Planet Mars
L ying around in my car
O ver and over at Mars
R acing each other to the moon
A gain, can't we go home soon?
T o the top of Mars
I n our space cars
O n Saturn, can we have an ice cream?
N o, because we are flying through a beam!

Victory Turner (10)
St George's Cathedral Catholic Primary School, Southwark

Space Aliens

Aliens are kind
But they have a strange mind
While being miserable and scared
They often smile and care

Aliens are bizarre and very fast
But they would never end up in a cast
They aliens can really walk
But really, can they talk?

Aliens had been in a rocket
But they have an unknown pocket
While they're eating dust and air
Don't you think about it, because I do care!

Janelle Koyabanzoua (10)
St George's Cathedral Catholic Primary School, Southwark

Gloomy Loomy

Aliens do not eat lollies
They eat sweets
Why do they eat because...
I don't know - ah! I remember
Because they like it but
They say planets are really crazy
And stars are so bright
That you can go blind
There is gravity everywhere
We fly like birds
And sometimes we go to the moon
The perfect circle in space
Sometimes we wonder
What a fantastic adventure
In space.

Leonor Aynoa Alvarez (9)
St George's Cathedral Catholic Primary School, Southwark

Outer Space

Stars shine so bright
Looking at this beautiful sight
Amazing alien as always
Earth, usual as known

Mars which is close to the stars
The dark breathtaking moon
One day you may see it soon
The black hole called the unknown

Gravity, growing, gone
The brave star traveller
Planets, people, places
This is what it's like in outer space.

Ngozi Esther Onuh-Reuben (9)
St George's Cathedral Catholic Primary School, Southwark

Planets

P lenty of time goes throughout planets
L etting us know that no one could live there
A s comets fly by through the galactic dark
N ever-ending stars make a never-ending mark
E very star that ever goes there
T akes another face of beauty, which couldn't spare
S pace is an unbelievable and never-ending fair.

Jhin Orozco (10)
St George's Cathedral Catholic Primary School, Southwark

Saturn In The Solar System

S pace is unbelievable and just never-ending
A stronauts from NASA they will be sending
T V shows about space are going to be trending
U ranus is the neighbour we call it the gas giant
R ound rings go round the planet with dust
N ow it is the end, learn the planets, you must!

Abolaji Bamidele - Alao (9)
St George's Cathedral Catholic Primary School, Southwark

Explore

E nter the freezing world of planets
X ylophones can't make a lovely tune
P lanets all shapes and sizes
L ots like Mars, Venus, Earth and the moon
O r just follow the lead of Neil Armstrong
R evisiting might be long
E xplore and have so much fun.

Chryssa Dionson (10)
St George's Cathedral Catholic Primary School, Southwark

Planets In Space

P luto is a dwarf planet
L anding on the bright shining moon
A stronauts landing on flaming hot Mars
N eptune is a planet in our solar system
E arth supports life
T ravelling through cosmic space
S pace is full of different planets.

Catherine Michael (10)
St George's Cathedral Catholic Primary School, Southwark

Planets

P luto is a dwarf planet
L ife somewhere but unknown
A ll planets rotate around the sun
N ow they have all shown
E ach planet is ordered well
T he biggest star above
S pace is a wonder that can't be undone.

Ahrienne Lucia Dizon Custodio (10)
St George's Cathedral Catholic Primary School, Southwark

Aliens Are Interesting To Learn About

Splish splash
Splu
Aliens are interesting!
Splish splash
Splu
Aliens are slimy!
Splish splash
Splu
Aliens are weird!
Splish splash
Splu
Aliens are travellers!
Splish splash
Splu.

Daniel Perez Arteaga (10)
St George's Cathedral Catholic Primary School, Southwark

Space

Haiku poetry

Universe is void
It is exciting and cold
See lots of planets

When exploring it
You see many twinkling stars
They are beautiful

You have Mercury
And many more planets shine
It is galactic.

Esther Kamande (10)
St George's Cathedral Catholic Primary School, Southwark

Space

The planets were in circles
And the aliens were slimy
The stars were shiny
And there was no gravity
So we were flying around
Seeing the planets in circles
Slimy aliens and shiny stars.

Allison Nicole Rey Arriaga (10)
St George's Cathedral Catholic Primary School, Southwark

Scary Aliens

A ngry scary aliens
L onely scary aliens
I nvading scary aliens
E nvious scary aliens
N ameless scary aliens
S limy scary aliens.

Jesus Marquez (10)
St George's Cathedral Catholic Primary School, Southwark

Space Alien

Star-watcher
Mars-visitor
Rocket-launcher
Revolting features
Unknown ruler
Ice cream-lover
What does that matter?
It's an alien!

Samuela Sesay (10)
St George's Cathedral Catholic Primary School, Southwark

Space

S pacious space
P eculiar aliens in space
A stronaut about in space
C hilly planets
E ternal Earth.

Denis Santiago Daza (9)
St George's Cathedral Catholic Primary School, Southwark

Space

S olar systems are made up of many planets
P luto is the smallest planet made up of rock and ice
A stronauts conduct experiments in space
C apsules are used when astronauts come back to Earth
E arth can be seen from space.

Kymeila Henry (7)
St Joseph's Primary School, Gabalfa

The Big Bang

In this world
Jolly people sang
School bells rang
And passers by spoke slang

Nearby on the street
People came to meet
Some took a seat
And the rest ate some meat

On the land
People played with sand
Some made food by hand
And the rest were all banned

And then there was a big... *bang!*

Sharinie Sriharan (9)
Whitchurch Primary School & Nursery, Stanmore

Weather Crew

Weather, weather, where are you
We are the weather crew
We look for you everywhere
But all we find is a piece of pear
It's like you're naughty as a monkey
So don't get angry because that's not fair
We see you go as hard as you blow
But you don't realise so go, go, go.

Isha Sanghvi (8)
Whitchurch Primary School & Nursery, Stanmore

Lonely

Roses aren't red
Violets aren't blue
No one will be there
No not for you

Even when you cry
Even when you scream
If someone's there
It will be in your dreams

People say tomorrow will be a better day
Laughing, dancing, everything's fake
They put on a fake smile
Even though they know
What's happened to me is pretty life-changing
I loved her lots and now she's gone
Oh why oh why oh why.

Lola Moffatt (11)
Yattendon School, Horley

YOUNG WRITERS INFORMATION

We hope you have enjoyed reading this book – and that you will continue to in the coming years.

If you're a young writer who enjoys reading and creative writing, or the parent of an enthusiastic poet or story writer, do visit our website **www.youngwriters.co.uk**. Here you will find free competitions, workshops and games, as well as recommended reads, a poetry glossary and our blog. There's lots to keep budding writers motivated to write!

If you would like to order further copies of this book, or any of our other titles, then please give us a call or order via your online account.

Young Writers
Remus House
Coltsfoot Drive
Peterborough
PE2 9BF
(01733) 890066
info@youngwriters.co.uk

Join in the conversation!
Tips, news, giveaways and much more!

YoungWritersUK   @YoungWritersCW